BREAKOUT BRAND

Breakout Brand: 30 days to your Personal and Business Power Brand
© Copyright 2018 by Walt Laurel
ISBN-13: 978-1726173537
ISBN-10: 1726173534

Passion Driven Marketing
Clearwater, Florida 33759
Email: support@PassionDrivenMarketing.com

All Rights Reserved. No part of this publication may be reproduced, distributed, transmitted in any form or by any means, including photocopying, recording or other electronic or mechanical methods, or by any information storage retrieval system without the prior written permission of the publisher and author except in the case of brief quotations embodied in critical reviews and certain other non-commercial uses permitted by copyright law.

Book interior design by Jean Boles
jean.bolesbooks@gmail.com

BREAKOUT BRAND

30 Days to your Personal and Business Power Brand

WALT LAUREL

DEDICATION

This book is dedicated to those who have stood by me in my journey that included many high and low moments in my life.

In particular, I'd like to thank my wonderful wife, "Jett" for being the love of my life, my greatest fan, best friend, and sometimes most demanding coach. ☺

To my mom and dad for instilling the principles of hard work, dedication, service to country, and the value of family throughout my life, military career, and business ventures.

To my grandad, uncles and other proud military men who paved the way for me and countless others, providing us with the opportunities that we have today, despite oftentimes encountering demeaning and degrading conditions on the home front yourselves. You all stood tall and paved the path with dignity, honor, and service!

With Love,

Walt

CONTENTS

PREFACE 11
   Living Life on Your Own Terms... 11
CHAPTER ONE 17
   Introduction... 17
      POWER PRINCIPLE: Leaders build personal and business power brands! 21
      POWER PRINCIPLE: Building and leveraging your personal and business power brand should never be unethical.. 24
CHAPTER TWO... 27
   The Power of a Power Brand.. 27
CHAPTER THREE 31
   Your Inner Brand 31
      POWER PRINCIPLE: Unique Core Values 31
      POWER PRINCIPLE: Your Brand is created from the inside (your core) out (how others see you), not the other way around. 32
      POWER PRINCIPLE: Power Branders serve a mission greater than themselves! 36
CHAPTER FOUR.. 41
   Dress for Results 41
      POWER PRINCIPLE: Power Branders dress for results. 41

CHAPTER FIVE 47
   Confidence vs. Competence 47
CHAPTER SIX 55
   Authenticity 55
      POWER PRINCIPLE: Authenticity 55
      POWER PRINCIPLE: Power Branders are authentic in words and actions 56
      POWER PRINCIPLE: Power Branders are doers, not just talkers 57
CHAPTER SEVEN 61
   Accountability 61
      POWER PRINCIPLE: Accountability 61
      POWER PRINCIPLE: Power Branders do not make excuses and are accountable for their actions and results! 63
CHAPTER EIGHT 67
   Relevance 67
      POWER PRINCIPLE: Relevance 67
      POWER PRINCIPLE: Power Branders study, learn, apply and refine. 69
CHAPTER NINE 73
   Power Networks and Relationships 73
      POWER PRINCIPLE: Establish powerful networks and relationships 73
      POWER PRINCIPLE: Power Branders in company settings devote dedicated time to reach up, down, and across the company to foster critical relationships. 77

CHAPTER TEN	79
Action	79
POWER PRINCIPLE: Take Action Now!	79
CHAPTER ELEVEN	83
Repairing Brand Damage	83
CHAPTER TWELVE	89
Bonus! How to Turbocharge your Power Brand	89
COACHING AND CONSULTING	93
A Note from the Author	93
ABOUT THE AUTHOR	95

PREFACE

Living Life on Your Own Terms

One of the biggest misconceptions we learn when we're growing up is that we, somehow, are guided by some universal principle that determines what our life will be, and in some cases, our ability to live where we want—and the biggest lie of them all, how much money we will make. That's the misconception of the "silver spoon."

If you're not born with some fictitious silver spoon, all hope is lost!

Walt Laurel

I know when I was a little kid growing up, one of the things I was told is, "go to school get a good job, find a nice company, and stay with that company until you retire."

Sounded good at the time...

Little did I realize at the time—of course, I was probably seven or eight years old—that they were really talking about living in the same place, and doing the same thing, for 20 or 30 years and retiring "happy."

Now, don't get me wrong, the people advising me when I was young were all great people. Warm-hearted, hard-working wonderful people who instilled a lot of the values in me that I have to this very day. But one of the things I did find out as I was growing up and getting older was that those statements were absolutely not true.

Let's talk about YOU for a second.

Wouldn't you like to take control of your career and steer it in the direction that you want it to go?

Wouldn't you like to live where you want to live? Not where you are forced to live?

Wouldn't you like to live life on YOUR own terms?

Of course you would!

Well, one of the things that I've found through a number of decades of time consuming and costly trial and error is the ability to answer all of those questions...Hell, yah!

How?

Breakout Brand:
30 days to your Personal and Business Power Brand

I've found that being able to have a Personal Power Brand is something that has allowed me flexibility to live where I want to live, to do the things that I want to do, to not feel stuck in any situation that I'm in, and to…have choices!

Those choices become a new reality for you and allow you to expand into other things, such as owning your own business or running a not-for-profit, spending more time in a charitable endeavor, giving back to the community, and having more time to spend with your family and loved ones.

But it all starts with understanding one key principle. Just one.

You deserve more!

I know that sounds like some personal development double-talk, but it's really not.

So think about it.

What are the things that you really want <u>right now</u>?

Would you like to:

- Spend more time doing what you want to do?
- Grow to a higher position in your current career?
- Move on to something different, a different line of work or a different career?
- Start your own small business?
- Be an entrepreneur and live the laptop lifestyle?

Those things are all possible, but everything starts with YOUR Personal and Business Power Brand!

Warning: What you may think are your BS detectors going off right now are nothing more than the self-limiting inner voice that may be holding you back from moving forward in your career and life.

If you want more and know you deserve more, it's time to declare:

"I deserve more AND I'm willing to take action to get it!"

You have a unique set of knowledge, skills, capabilities, and desires that when channeled correctly will enable you to take control of your current situation and move you to new levels that you may not even realize or can imagine. Until now!

What if I told you that following a simple, straightforward formula can move you from where you are now to where you want to be in just 30 days?

So, why thirty days?

Thirty days is long enough for you to make a firm decision that you deserve more, digest what's in this short book, take action and make a difference in your life, career, and business.

I deliberately made this book short, actionable and easy to digest. It's the size that it needs to be to be effective. Most people (not you, of course ☺) simply do not finish the books they start; they get bogged down in details and never take action on what they read. Simple fact.

Breakout Brand:
30 days to your Personal and Business Power Brand

"Here's my guarantee to you...if you take thirty short days following this step-by-step blueprint, commit to the process (hey, it's only 30 days!), you will get the results you want along with allowing yourself the opportunity to chart your own course in the future!"

*Disclaimer: You have to be a person of action. If you're not a person of action, it's probably best that you still read this book, because it may be the wake-up call that you need to move forward if you've found yourself in a rut and you don't really know how to get out. But for the rest of us, and I know you're one of them, it is time for you to take action—NOW.

This is a **SPRINT**—not a marathon—designed to infuse a quick burst of enthusiasm, momentum, and results for you that will also provide a foundation for future success. As you will see throughout the book, winners are sprinters!

That's the world we live in, given the pace of change being at a staggering level that will continue from now on. Gone are the days of "slow and steady" wins the race. This book is designed for YOU to win every race, every time!

Action steps: Read the book and go through the exercises to obtain the status of…

The Power Brander!

This is your 30-day call to action!

Let's get going…

CHAPTER ONE

Introduction

Brand: *A Unique design ('you"), sign, symbol, words, or a combination of these, employed in creating an image that identifies and differentiates you from your competitors. Over time, this image becomes associated with a level of credibility, quality, and satisfaction in the observer's mind.*

As you can see there are a few key words that define a **brand:**

- Unique
- Differentiates
- Credibility

- Quality
- Satisfaction in the observer's mind

I know you've been told the myth that branding is something for large companies, the fortune 500's, that it's something that entrepreneurs and career professionals as well as small business owners shouldn't really have to worry about. Why?

- Myth 1: It takes a huge marketing and advertising budget.
- Myth 2: It takes an entire marketing team.
- Myth 3: (And even more important to you), it's not something that's important to move forward in your career, be successful as an entrepreneur, nor grow your small business.

Well, let me tell you, nothing can be further from the truth.

Remember our definition of **brand**?

Unique - You are definitely unique, there is no other you.

Differentiates - You have a unique combination of skills that no one else has.

Credibility – The combination of what you say vs. what you do.

Quality – You bring that to all you do, no shortcuts or excuses.

Satisfaction in the observer's mind – You perform with a standard of excellence as viewed by others.

Whether you realize it or not, you have a personal and business brand!

You're probably asking yourself at this point...

Breakout Brand:
30 days to your Personal and Business Power Brand

What is a "Power Brand?"

I want you to think of a Power Brand as the combination of three critical things:

1. How you see or view yourself

2. What actions you take—actions do speak louder than words

3. How others see or view you

Make no mistake, ALL of the three have to be in alignment.

So what's the big deal about your personal or your business Power Brand?

I remember when I was a brand new, fresh out of college, US Naval Officer reporting to my first ship, the *USS Nassau*. Imagine a young, headstrong guy who thought he was God's gift to the US Navy.

I knew I had the world at my feet. I mean, think about it, an engineering graduate, a distinguished graduate of two US Naval schools that prepared me (or at least I thought so) to be able to step in day one and take charge. Imagine me walking down the pier, staring up at this HUGE Naval vessel, thinking, "Gosh, I can't wait to go in and just take charge." I was not lacking in confidence. As I walked on board they greeted me with, "Welcome aboard Mr. Laurel, welcome to the finest ship in the Navy."

"Wait a minute; did he just call me Mr.... Laurel?"

I thought, "Now, I know I'm the Man!"

Walt Laurel

I was taken to where my sleeping quarters would be (called a "stateroom" for Officers in the Navy—"A Stateroom! Now I've really arrived!")—and introduced that same morning to my unit: 25 hard-charging sailors who I thought were ready to listen to my every word and move at my every command, along with two senior enlisted personnel, and a more senior noncommissioned officer—the Chief.

Immediately, I began to start barking orders and commands based on the training that I had gotten, because that's what I thought I was supposed to do. I was the MAN, right?

Well, you can imagine, here I was thinking that I was God's gift to the US Navy, while the actions I was taking were those of—quite frankly—the brand new jerk.

Little did I know that behind my back the words and term that was used for young, brash know-it-all officers like myself, was "N-Swine." That's right, I was no longer Ensign Laurel, I was now N-Swine Laurel, which was a really derogatory and well-deserved new name!

I remember passing a few of my troops one day and hearing them laugh about the new N-Swine. Sadly, it took a while for me to realize that my personal brand was horrible. I had missed the boat (pun intended) on the three key things that create a power brand:

1. How I perceived myself---Okay that one was good.☺
2. The actions I took—Quite simply, I was a jerk to others.
3. How others perceived me—"That guy is a jerk!"

Needless to say, it took a long time for me to recover and build a Power Brand. I don't know how many hours I spent trying to live down the initial impression I made. Eventually, as my sailors saw that I was willing to take on the tough assignments, stand side by side with them in the not-so-fun activities aboard a naval vessel at sea, and most importantly, stand up for them in difficult situations, my brand (and real name☺) was recovered!

Reminder: **ALL** three of those have to be in alignment for you to have a power brand.

If we take a look at what's going on in the constantly changing, dynamic business and professional environment that we now live in and what we're looking at in the future, it's absolutely critical that you look at what your current personal and business power brand is and even more important—how you leverage your personal and business Power Brand to **guarantee** success.

Contrary to most books about brand, this book is about **YOU!**

Throughout the book, you will also be introduced to power brand and leadership principles that are key to building, leveraging, and living your Power Brand. At this point you may be asking yourself...

"Leadership? What in the heck does that have to do with branding?"

> **POWER PRINCIPLE: Leaders build personal and business power brands!**

Perhaps you've never considered yourself a leader, you've never been in typical leadership positions, or you've told yourself the biggest myth of them all, namely, "Leaders are born, not made."

As if there was some universal game of duck, duck, goose* or musical chairs* that determines who is born to be a leader. Sounds absurd doesn't it!

To that I declare for you---bull dookey!

Keep reading and I will debunk that theory once and for all, free you to become the leader you can be, and share with you the secrets to building your unique power brand.

Fair enough?

Well, who am I? And why should you even care?

You see, I've also struggled with the idea of the importance of my personal and business brand, first as a US Naval Officer fresh out of college, ready to take on the world, then as a professional in a number of Fortune 500 brand leading companies, and as a small business owner and serial entrepreneur.

Gone are the days of simply showing up, doing what you're told, making small incremental career steps and hoping for the best.

In the new age, it's time to stand up, break out of the crowd, and finally take control of your own unique personal and business power brand.

That, my friend, is what this book is about.

Breakout Brand:
30 days to your Personal and Business Power Brand

30 Days to Your personal and Business Power Brand!

So why did I write this book?

There are so many dynamic things going on in the world in which we find ourselves. We've got technology exploding around us at an ever-increasing pace, with shorter duration from one "breakthrough" to another—thus allowing the career professional to be more efficient and effective.

Sounds great, doesn't it?

Well, not so fast! Technology is no longer a key distinguisher in career progression. Everybody can leverage the same technology…easy to acquire, easy to learn how to use, and easy to deploy in the workplace.

You also have the greatest opportunity that you've ever had to become an entrepreneur and start your own business, in many instances with little or no money down.

Seems great doesn't it?

Again, not so fast…the flipside of that is that there are so many great people (like you) who are doing the same. So how do you stand up and break out?

You have the opportunity to grow your career in a dynamic way. But there's one big *however* in here.

And that is, "How do you position yourself?"

You see, branding is really about positioning; it's how you distinguish yourself from the people you work with, or other entrepreneurs and business owners who are trying to be as effective or competitive as you are. There's no doubt that the competition (and that's what it is!) is tough, but I truly believe you can leverage these principles to always come out on top.

Caution!

There's a number of ways to do that. Some of them are underhanded or could be even thought to be unethical. But that's not the reason for this book, nor is it something that I would even suggest you do.

POWER PRINCIPLE: Building and leveraging your personal and business power brand should never be unethical.

Now, this book is going to be very straightforward and to the point; there's no need to beat around the bush or to add a lot of fluff. I hope you appreciate getting down to business and making this work for you personally, in your career and/or in your business success.

Just another warning: What you will receive in the next chapters are real world principles that will seem contrary to what you've seen or read about branding in most, if not all, "business books." The good news is that building or refining your Power Brand can be accomplished in 30 days or less.

So what's the catch?

Simple: You have to be willing to open your mind, be honest to yourself, and most importantly:

TAKE ACTION!

Breakout Brand:
30 days to your Personal and Business Power Brand

So here's where magic for you begins. You see, the reason I wrote this book is because there is a lot of myths, misconceptions, and lies in the marketplace that are trying to get you to believe that you can't really build a brand as a career professional, entrepreneur or a small business owner, which is totally false.

The reason I know this first hand is that I've literally spent over two decades creating and recreating my own brand, first as an Officer in the US Navy, then at a number of Fortune 500 companies in over 20 plus years of leadership roles, as a radio show host of a highly successful and empowering show, as well as a serial entrepreneur and small business owner myself.

My success is **easily repeatable** if you are willing to break out of your current mode and embrace a power brand for yourself!

The good news for you is that you don't have to relive all of the trial and error, brand blunders, and restarts that I personally had to live through. We'll get to share and have some fun with many of those in the coming chapters.

Here are the 9 Power Brand Principles that define a *Power Brander* (yes, that's a new title that I made up☺) and will skyrocket your success, enable you to be the authentic, unique you, and position you to live life on your own terms:

- Your Unique Core Values
- A Mission larger than you
- Dress for Results
- Authenticity
- Accountability

- Relevance
- Power Networks and Relationships (Law of Attraction)
- Confidence vs. Competence
- Action

I know you're ready, so let's jump right into "How do I create a Power Brand?"

CHAPTER TWO

The Power of a Power Brand

What's the big deal about having a power brand? We have already defined a brand as how you actually represent yourself to the world, or how the world actually sees you. It's an intersection of you and how you perceive yourself as well as how others perceive you. That's a really important point, but the bottom line here is, what are the benefits? The benefit of a power brand is that it allows you to determine things on *your own terms.*

Now think about that for a second. What would it be like for you to live where you want to live, for you to do what you want to do in your career, to work at the workplace—if that's what you'd like to do as a professional—whenever or wherever you want?

How about make more money?

How about the ability to impact and influence your career as well? If you're reading this book, you are definitely an entrepreneur or career professional that invests time into increasing your leadership, coaching, or business acumen. Wouldn't you like to leverage the learning while at the same time making a huge impact on your company, marketplace, or community?

Of course you do!

How about the flexibility to leave your current position, knowing you'd be highly sought after elsewhere, or knowing that you have the confidence to decide on your terms, that it's time to make a career or business market move. Let's say the market goes south like it did in 2008. I think the most important part, and the part that excites me the most—and I hope that it also excites you—is the ability to have a great work/life balance even in a stressful career or as an entrepreneur or a small business owner.

That is probably the most important thing for those who are very principle-centered leaders, whether they are in a corporate position, whether they're in an operational position, whether they're an entrepreneur, whether they're a small business owner in a family owned business. Maybe you're a franchisee, but the work/life balance, that is the thing that tends to be, in most cases, the killer. I've been blessed to be able to work both in corporate America as well as a private consultant.

Breakout Brand:
30 days to your Personal and Business Power Brand

I've lived in a number of different places that I particularly chose to live in. I spent more time with my family, including a few years home schooling my own son. More about that story as we get into the book a little bit further, but I've been able to enjoy doing the things that I love to do. I, myself, I love the water. I love fishing, diving—hey, come on, I'm a Navy guy, not too surprising, right? I've been able to travel to over 30 countries, and I've been able to enjoy that travel with my family and particularly to show my young children—young at the time—different places that many people never get to go to in their whole life.

But you know what? That's my story.

Your story should be based upon those things and those places and those opportunities that you want for you, for your family, your friends and those that you really care about. Again, it takes action, so now it's time for you to write your story in the next 30 days.

Let's get going.

CHAPTER THREE

Your Inner Brand

POWER PRINCIPLE: Unique Core Values

Who are you?

I know that's actually a crazy thing to ask.

It's obvious, you're going to probably say my name is (fill in the blank). But that's not really who you are or what makes you unique is it?

The first principle of power branding is being able to understand, and to leverage, your core values. I know this may not seem like it's something that really even applies to you as a unique individual because of the way that you perceive this concept called *brand*.

Contrary to what you may have read or heard:

> **POWER PRINCIPLE: Your Brand is created from the inside (your core) out (how others see you), not the other way around.**

Let's talk about your core values. Usually these are things like faith, family, friends, service, loyalty, trust, and honesty. There is no magic formula for what you, as a unique person, should define as your core values.

I was first introduced to this concept as a young man with the Cub Scouts:

> On my honor I will do my best
> To do my duty to God and my country
> And to obey the Scout Law;
> To help other people at all times;
> To keep myself physically strong,
> mentally awake, and morally straight.

Those things have been instilled in me from the time that I was young, growing up, to the time that I became an officer in the

Breakout Brand:
30 days to your Personal and Business Power Brand

US Navy, and have continued for the remainder of my corporate and business career, even till today.

Now, I've shortened it down to these four:

- Service
- Loyalty
- Trust
- Honesty

Take a second to step back and think about that. What are the things that you hold most valuable at your core or that help define you?

What are those values you hold sacred to your core?

Those values, that even when you are in a stressful situation, remain steadfast?

Take a few minutes; write down those two to three, perhaps four powerful things that define who you are and your unique core values.

Then, write down a defining statement that shows how you actually make those things happen or bring those things to life?

For example, if it's honesty, it would be something like, "I am honest in my business dealings, and I don't allow others around me to be dishonest."

Another example…Trust: "I instill trust in my core team, as well as the people who work with me, by being honorable and doing what I say I'm going to do."

Loyalty: "I'm loyal to those who share similar core values that I have; that includes my team, my business associates, as well as my family, my friends, and those whom I associate with socially."

Using those examples, go ahead and write a sentence or a few words that define what each one of your core values means to you. That's the *core* of what *keeps you grounded*, especially when you are confronted with a stressful situation.

There is no greater test of your core values than when you are subjected to a stressful situation.

Think about a time when you saw someone else (in a stressful situation) appear to miraculously transform from a dynamic, confident, caring man or woman to a total opposite mean-spirited ogre. You may have wondered…"Who in the hell is that?"

Happens all the time during times of stress when your real core values come to the surface!

In business, your core values are constantly put to the test. I have a number of examples, particularly when I was in the Navy, of people talking about certain things that they believe in. Then, as the famous phrase goes:

"You better watch what you do in the dark because it'll come out in the light."

People who are not firmly grounded in their core values oftentimes, in times of duress, are completely opposite to what they say their core values are.

Breakout Brand:
30 days to your Personal and Business Power Brand

Bottom line for you: **Power Branders embrace their unique set of core values that can withstand stressful situations!**

If you've defined your core values and are willing to commit to them, I'd like to congratulate you for being in the top 1% (hint: Power Branders are in the top 1%).

If not, I'd like for you to re-read this chapter because it's so important for the foundation of your Power Brand. OK, let's get it going; we only have 30 days!

"So now that I've done that Walt…what's next?"

POWER PRINCIPLE: A Mission Greater Than You

As a young man, I used to love sitting with my grandfather, listening to different stories about his youth, high school years, and then going off and enlisting in the US Navy. He always spoke of these times with pride, honor, and fondness that didn't necessarily reflect the issues he and other men of color faced during WWII, especially in the US Navy, as well as at home in the segregated South.

At that time, men of color were only allowed to function in the role of cooks aboard naval ships.

Important Note: I'm in no way disparaging our wonderful men and women who are serving in that role today….

The point is, that was the ONLY role available at that time for men of color.

Now, you probably would have thought that my grandfather's recollections would be sprinkled with some disdain for his individual treatment at home and abroad. Actually, it was quite the opposite!

I remember one day I asked him..."Grandad, why don't you tell me about some of the bad things or how "we" were treated back then in the Navy."

His simple response, which I can remember till this day, was..."I was serving for a mission greater than me."

To this day, that moment lives in me, strengthens my core values and is a foundation for my life.

POWER PRINCIPLE: Power Branders serve a mission greater than themselves!

That's a true definition of your mission.

Your mission is that what you desire to give to the world.

Caution: if you've never thought about it, it may seem like a strange concept to you, but let's give it a shot, and I'll also share mine with you.

Here goes: My mission is to "lead, teach, and empower business professionals and entrepreneurs in order to make a difference in the world."

That's it. That's my gift to the world; that's the same mission that I've had for the last two decades or more, once I was introduced to the concept of my personal mission.

Breakout Brand:
30 days to your Personal and Business Power Brand

At this point your inner voice may be asking...what does this have to do with branding?

Let me introduce you to a concept called **congruence**, which is nothing more than "agreement, or harmony, or being in a state of harmony."

As a business professional, when you find that your core values and mission are congruent and in alignment with the company you work for, clients you serve, or your market, you're uniquely positioned to build your power brand and to be successful.

In other words, you're all in alignment. You're all in congruence. I'll give you a hint here. It is also a key to establishing and building key relationships. Congruence is a very important part of any type of relationship that you have with either another person or another entity.

Let me give you an example about congruence. Back in the late '70s to early '80s, Johnson & Johnson, a wonderful company with a rich history in the US market, had a Tylenol scare. There were a number of product tampering cases that brought into light that there were some issues with how the company's product packaging was. Once the cases were discovered, the company had two choices that they could undertake to address the issues:

- Number one: They could run away from it, they could hide it, or they could do a lot of things to keep it out of the media and hidden from the public.
- Number two: They could go back to their core values and company mission and face it head on.

The CEO at that time took the bold move of making sure that the American public, the media, the doctors and nurses that depended on the J&J brand, as well as the company shareholders, were completely informed as to what had occurred.

So what did he do? He came out and publicly called for a recall of all of the Tylenol product. Now if you think about it, that's a lot of product, and it turned out to cost hundreds of millions of dollars in the effort. As a matter of fact, he had to do it over a number of different occasions. One of the obvious after effects was a significant drop in the stock price and loss in market value.

Now, if you were to look back at the history of Johnson & Johnson, if you had remained faithful to the company and held your stock as a stockholder, your return on your investment since that time would have multiplied many, many times over.

So what does this have to do with congruence? The company aligned its core values with its mission, which further enhanced the brand. So, as an entrepreneur, small business owner, or business professional, two of the core principles in building and maintaining your Power Brand are:

- Having a unique set of core values
- Having alignment (congruence) with a mission that is greater than yourself

Now, it's your turn....What is your mission, your gift to the world? Is it aligned to your core values?

Here's a few of examples for you to use:

- "I want to empower 1000 entrepreneurs to become millionaires."
- "I want to provide education to women in impoverished countries."
- "I want to bring water to drought-infested countries, solve particular health crises, or provide for homeless veterans,"

Go ahead, give it a shot!

CHAPTER FOUR

Dress for Results

POWER PRINCIPLE: Power Branders dress for results.

After graduating from college, it was off to the Navy. I remember as I was about to report onboard, I was given a checklist of a number of items to be placed into my sea bag that would represent the uniforms that I would have for my time aboard the ship. When I looked inside, it was quite strange to me to see that I would have multiple pairs of the same items. At the time, I thought it was a little bit peculiar and perhaps there'd be something else that I needed to get when I was onboard.

So fast forward to the time that I step on board in my nice dress white uniform, ready to take on the world. Immediately I was told "Take off your dress whites, Ensign Laurel; put on your khakis and let's go to work."

Needless to say, that was the uniform of the day....every day, unless there was something special going on, for the next six months. Why six months?

Every six months we would change into a different seasonal uniform. I remember wearing (not the same outfit) but the same colors, the same branding, the same everything for our six-month deployments. The reason, of course, was for team and unit cohesion and unity (result) of a common uniform, common cause.

As I was transitioning from military service to a new career in the corporate sector, I, like many other junior military officers, enlisted the service of an executive recruiter who was especially adept at getting junior military officers placed in some of the most popular and prestigious companies, based on our leadership and management experience, matched with the **core values** that most successful military officers possessed. As I began to work with the recruiter, I was told, "You have to get a power suit in order to impress the potential employers you'll be interviewing with!"

I think a lot of us remember it—the power suit. It's the pinstriped suit (men and women), pressed white shirt, red power tie, and shiny black shoes. For men, it was oxford shoes, as I recall.

Wow. Now you're ready!

That was the suit I used in my interview that landed me my first position with Johnson and Johnson---recall our power principle of core values. That was the norm for *dress for success* as well as similar suits for many years. Then came the advent of what was called "Casual Friday."

Casual Friday allowed you to dress down on Friday's, usually jeans, or a polo shirt…Wow, what a difference! Now you can actually dress down a little bit on Fridays. Perhaps wear those khaki pants or a pair of trousers and a golf shirt or an oxford shirt, or something like that.

Fast forward to today. We are witnessing the rise of an amazing array of technology companies, as well as other companies that are deploying casual "creative (at times)" dress norms. Where everything is about collaboration, and you can wear casual wear at all times—things like shorts and jeans, which were never even heard of back when I first began my business career.

So what are YOU as a Power Brander supposed to do?

POWER PRINCIPLE: Power Branders dress for results.

For you, as a career business professional, recall that one of the key aspects of a power brand is how people see or perceive you. A lot is based on the first impression of you by others. Here's a quote that has remained ingrained in me for many years,

"You never get a second chance at a first impression!"

Although I realize for you in particular, the company that you work with may be a "casual dress" company, and it may be perfectly <u>acceptable and encouraged</u> to casually dress at all times, but there will be those times when you probably want to show that your brand brings authority, control, and power positioning. In those cases, you will want to wear a suit or something above the norm, because that will make you stand out.

Here are some scenarios where Power Branders dress for results:

- Internal interviews---obvious, but I had to mention it. There is nothing worse than an internal candidate that shows up to an interview with casual attire. Don't do it!
- When you're interviewing candidates for your team
- Key presentations—remember no second chances at first impressions
- Key external vendor / supplier visits
- First formal one-on-one meeting with a new boss

Don't let the casual dress style ruin your opportunity to continue to build your Power Brand!

For entrepreneurs and online business owners it's really very simple. Your outer brand is your website and your social media presence. For a small business owner, it's your storefront and how your physical location looks. It's how your employees interact with customers. It's how your employees or your help desk responds to your website's support requests. All those things are part of your outer brand. It may be time for:

- A website makeover
- Update of your social media profile

Breakout Brand:
30 days to your Personal and Business Power Brand

- ➤ Brand makeover of your marketing materials
- ➤ Revision to the dress standards and standard operating procedures of your employees (for business owners)

Bottom line to you: Power branders dress for results.

Which means that you're good at knowing those situations when a higher standard of dress is called for. Don't be the person who is wearing something that looks like you're supposed to go to a 60s revival for Woodstock or a disco revival from the '70s, when in fact, you should be wearing your power dress attire.

At this point, your inner voice may be saying... "But Walt, it's about individuality, self-expression, you know, a creative environment!"

Let me be clear, your inner voice is feeding you a line of BS!

The problem with that thinking is that if you're a **Power Brander**, and you want to elevate your Power Brand, you have to be able to dress the part and dress for results, which means that oftentimes you have to take control of the situation and stand out!

What people will see from you on the outside is often what they think they're going to get from you. So don't fool yourself into believing that you can go in to any business situations dressed like you are heading to a 60's reunion for Woodstock and think that you're going to be taken seriously right from the beginning.

The minimum standard doesn't apply to you because you are a Power Brander, and as such, you want to take it up a notch. Time to honestly assess how YOU dress for results. Take a look at the scenarios we discussed earlier in this chapter and how you were dressed...Be honest!

Did it help or hurt your Power Brand?

CHAPTER FIVE

Confidence vs. Competence

Let's talk about confidence versus competence. Confidence is defined as "the feeling of self-assurance arising from one's appreciation of one's own abilities or qualities" whereas competence is "the ability to do something successfully, efficiently or the way we want to do it at the highest level."

The other thing that we need to talk is a paradigm shift. A paradigm is a framework, or the way that we look at, and the way we see things.

There's a powerful quote by Dr. Wayne Dyer, "When you change the way you look at things, the things you look at change." I've often referred to this when I've challenged myself to think out of the box, consider new alternatives, or turn a perception upside down to create a new reality for me as well as my team.

What I'm challenging you to do is to take a look at how you perceive y*our competence versus your confidence.*

Let's get started...

When you look at confidence versus competence, there are four zones. Those zones go from low to high in your ability as well as your confidence to execute some of those things that enhance your career or business.

For example:

Zone one: Low confidence and low competence.

We call that the **opportunity zone,** and the reason that we call it the opportunity zone is because, quite frankly, you have the opportunity to grow your confidence in your particular career field, whether you're an entrepreneur or small business owner and you're talking about marketing or sales, budgeting, those kind of things. If you're in a corporate environment, your confidence to lead teams. Perhaps you have a sales team or a marketing team or you have an operations team. You obviously have to understand how those operations work or how your sales and marketing systems work. When you first start out, you may have low confidence.

The other thing that you probably have in zone one is low competence. That's why it's called an opportunity zone. You're not very confident about those things that you want to execute. Oftentimes, you don't know what you don't know. Obviously, *you're not in your power zone* and there are some things that you're going to have to do to move yourself forward. First, determine what you can quickly do to beef up on those areas where expertise in the topic is needed. We live in the Information Age, where knowledge of any particular topic is available with a simple "google" search. If you're a business professional, start with the company's strategic goals, as well as those objectives at the team level. Take advantage of the educational material already available on the given topic and enhance that with external research. You want to move to the Power Brand zone, so it's going to take some effort!

Let's move on to the next zone.

Zone two: High confidence and low competence.

We call this the **challenge zone**. You have a high level of confidence that, yes, you can execute at a high level, whether you're in a corporate setting, in an operational setting, whether you're an entrepreneur or whether you're a small business owner. You feel that high level of confidence that you have can get results.

However, your competence is very low. You don't have the experience. You don't necessarily have the knowledge, nor do you have the capability that would put you in a higher competency zone. On the flipside, that is probably one of the best jumping off points for you to determine how you're going to get to your Power Brand. The one thing here, and a big caution, is that you may be considered a newbie, and the other caution for you is to avoid the idea of "fake it till you make it," which is absolute crap!

Caution: Too often I see well-intentioned professionals take this approach and get labelled as *bullshit artists*. I know that may appear a bit strong on the language, but you do not want to fall prey to that trap.

Be authentic, recognize that you have a lot to learn in a short amount of time and take action.

Here's an example...have you ever gone to an event or presentation where the main speaker comes in, and they're well dressed and looking like an expert or authority. They look like they absolutely have it together. They exude confidence as they walk into the room, and as soon as they open their mouth, you know that what's coming out is nothing but crap. What I would caution you against is being one of those people, simply because people see through that ruse rather quickly.

Power tip: Take the time to quickly ramp up your competence in areas that you need to—leadership, team building, a technical area—wherever the gap exists. Do it quickly!

Zone three: Low confidence, but high competence—I call it the ***scholarly zone.***

You've probably met other professionals in this zone who exude a high level of competence and knowledge. You know that they know the subject matter backwards and forwards, up and down. However, if you ask them to get in front of a room of people or to present that to another group of people, it's very difficult for them and sometimes it just tears them apart. Here's a challenge, if you find yourself in this situation.

Breakout Brand:
30 days to your Personal and Business Power Brand

You need to be able to get beyond yourself, which is why we started with what are those core values that you have. What are those things that are part of your mission that you want to give to the world? If you are to be able to execute on those, you have to get out of that box that you're in and jump into that zone of high competence. For those who think that you can't do that in 30 days, there're plenty of ways for you to do so. There are things like going to different presentations and networking events, partnering with other people you trust who are good at presentations or public speaking. Organizations like Toastmasters provide a safe supportive atmosphere where you can gain confidence in your ability to present in front of other people—because you have the knowledge. You have the ability to do this, so get out there and make it happen. Think BIG, start small, and your confidence will continue to build.

Let's talk about the sweet spot. The sweet spot occurs when you have high confidence and high competence. That is:

Zone four: High confidence with high competence, aka the **Power Zone.**

Most Power Branders live in the zone of high confidence and high competence. How do you get there? One of the most important things is making sure that you're a student of constant learning. Another extremely important consideration, especially if you are in leadership position, is to have a high level of confidence; along with a high level of competence within your area of expertise. If someone were to ask you to dig beyond the surface knowledge of your area of expertise, you have to display a deeper understanding than most. That, my friend, is a Power Brand, and that's the place you want to be operating!

Let's summarize it really quickly.

- **Zone one: low confidence, low competence.** The *opportunity zone*. You've got some work to do in the next 30 days if you find yourself in that place. You're probably thought of as a newbie. Focus on gaining KSAs (Knowledge, Skills, and Abilities) in the key areas for your business success while investing time and energy in your ability to confidently execute.

- **Zone two: high confidence, low competence.** The *challenge zone*. You're out there, you feel it, you got the passion, but you just have to get the knowledge. One of the things that you should know that in 30 days, because of the ease of finding information, particularly on the internet, you can gain some level of competency at almost anything that you want. Don't let that stop you from thinking that you can't execute this 30-day challenge, because you absolutely can.

- **Zone three: low confidence, high competence.** The *scholarly zone*. In the next 30 days, leverage those strong KSAs you possess and invest quality time toward increasing your confidence and ability to "own the room," even if you are shy, introverted, or uncomfortable speaking in front of a small or large group currently.

- **Zone four: the *Power Zone*.** This is where you want to be as a Power Brander. High confidence with high competence! You can get there in the next 30 days regardless of what other zone that you start in. Will it take effort on your part? Absolutely! Is it worth it? Hell yes!

Breakout Brand:
30 days to your Personal and Business Power Brand

That's the zone that offers you freedom, flexibility, and control of your options. It allows you to live life on your terms in order to execute to your core values, and to live your core values the way that you want to, as well as execute to the mission that you described earlier on.

That requires you to take action and get moving during the next 30 days—no excuses!

CHAPTER SIX

Authenticity

POWER PRINCIPLE: Authenticity

Wikipedia defines authenticity as "a degree to which one is true to one's own personality, spirit or character despite external pressures."

Imagine that you are in a room full of people at a networking, business, or social event. After a while, you begin to notice small groups huddling around certain participants as if there was some magnetic force drawing people to them. As you get closer to one of the groups, you overhear something that the speaker says, something that seems very odd to you that makes you shake your head. This person is obviously "inflating the truth" at best, and to put it mildly, obviously trying to be someone whom they're not! That initial attraction now turns to something even more repulsive, so you decide to move to another group.

At the next group you notice the "mood in the air" is light, jovial, upbeat, as the focal person engages the small group, encouraging collaboration, discussing previous failures, along with their business or career wins. She is creating a sense of win-win for the entire group. You decide to join the group by addressing a few of them, who welcome you to the discussion.

So let me ask you, which of those two groups can you relate to the most?

I know, you'd take the second group every time!

> **POWER PRINCIPLE: Power Branders are authentic in words and actions**

The question I'd like for you to ask yourself is when the pressure is on or you're in the spotlight, who do you become?

Is it someone different than who you are on a daily basis?

Earlier on in the book, you defined your core values, those things that you hold as core to what you believe in and what you stand for. Take a moment and review those values you defined previously (you did do the exercise, didn't you?☺). What were the things that you decided were going to be your core values?

Those key items will serve as the foundation for your brand.

You then defined your mission, what you wanted to impart into the world—remember? A mission larger than *You*!

Reality check: There are a number of different types of people that we run in to in this world, and you've seen them. I'm sure you have. There are the talkers and then there are the doers. The talkers are those people that talk a good game, but when you take a look at how they execute on either their core values or on their mission or how they go about their daily execution of those things within their career or in their business, there's a total disconnect.

Because they talk a great game it's easy to be fooled into thinking that's how to succeed in business and in life, until you gage their actions and results. A lot of times there's no action there or the action that's taken does not even come close to living up to their talk.

Then there are the doers.

> **POWER PRINCIPLE: Power Branders are doers, not just talkers**

The doers are people who take decisive and authentic action, which leads to desired results.

We're going to talk a little later in the book about action in another one of the power principles, but at this point, ask yourself honestly, are you a talker or a doer?

Let me give you an example. As a young naval officer, one of the things that we did often aboard the ship was to do drills. In these drills we would practice how we would react in certain situations if the ship had a casualty, something catastrophic happened to the ship, there was a fire, there was flooding, or there was something else that went wrong with the ship and it became inoperable in certain different areas.

We practiced those scenarios again and again and again and again, until it was supposed to be second nature. Trust me, in a real situation aboard ship you don't have time to go get instructions or refer to a manual!

One of the things that I noticed was the difference between those young naval officers who were able to execute well when it came to drills, brag about how well they did, but then when it came down to the real thing, a lot of times you would find a totally different person. They'd appear to be in control. They'd be very firm in what they needed to execute in drills, but as soon as that real pressure turned on, they became more of a talker and less of a doer.

Power Branders on the other hand, are able to reach into those core values, along with their mission larger than themselves, and stay laser focused on the task at hand in spite of the external circumstances. After the exercise and drills, those Naval officers were the first to honestly critique their performance as well as the performance of their team in an *authentic* spirit of improvement. Those officers also outperformed their peers when it came down to an actual emergency at sea.

Here's the exercise that I'd like for you to do. In the next 7 days, I want you to share your inner core values and mission with at least three people. Why do I say three? Because you want to get a cross section of how others are perceiving you. You want to ask them some very simple questions. Most importantly, you want them to be honest, of course, about you and how they perceive you.

Preferably, you want to talk to those who are the doers versus the talkers. You'll want them to share with you how they see you in stressful situations. You've already put down what your core values are and you've determined what your mission is. What you want to do now is to determine how close your perception of yourself matches what others perceive, especially in stressful situations.

As you recall, a brand is not only the perception of yourself, but it's how others perceive you. So this exercise is just to see if the two perceptions match or if there's a disconnect. If the two match, then you know that you're operating with *authenticity*.

Caution: If your perception of you is not in agreement with how others perceive you, here's what you need to do immediately.

You have to determine how you can quickly close that gap. What are the positive steps you can immediately implement that will bring your words and deeds into alignment?

Remember, you've committed to achieving your Power Brand in 30 days, so there's not a lot time to sit around with your feelings hurt or to feel down about it.

It's time to get up and do something about it.

Remember, we only have 30 days. Let's get moving!

CHAPTER SEVEN

Accountability

POWER PRINCIPLE: Accountability

Early on in my military career, I was told something that became a core leadership principle for me throughout my military and business career:

"You can delegate responsibility, but you can never delegate accountability."

What is accountability?

"The **obligation** of an individual or organization to account for its activities, accept responsibility for them, and to disclose the results in a transparent manner. It also includes the responsibility for money or other entrusted property."

A few important parts of the definition of accountability include:

- Account for activities. Yes, you have to own what activities occur with your team, business associates, and employees.

- Disclose results in a transparent manner. **Power Branders are transparent in words and actions!**

- Includes money or other entrusted property. Business professionals, that includes assets placed in your care by your company or your business.

I remember how powerful a concept that was as I gained experience and rank and my units grew along with greater accountability. At the time I first entered the military I had never been accountable (nor responsible ☺) for anyone except me, so it was really strange for me to grasp the concept of being accountable for the men, women, and equipment of my military units.

When I was going through college and part of a fraternity (I know you're tempted to get a visual of the 70's movie, *Animal House* ☺), one of the things that was drilled into our memory was:

Breakout Brand:
30 days to your Personal and Business Power Brand

"Excuses are tools of the incompetent, used to build monuments to nothingness, and those who specialize in them are seldom good at anything else."

I've kept to that throughout my military career as well as in all of my corporate positions. And now, as an entrepreneur and business professional, I know that I am accountable for the results that come from not only mine but my teams' actions. The accountability bus stops here!

I'm accountable for how our customers, clients, and business partners are treated, as well as accountable for those actions that I take, representing my brand.

POWER PRINCIPLE: Power Branders do not make excuses and are accountable for their actions and results!

Power Branders are very aware of that. Does that mean that they don't make any mistakes? Of course, you will make mistakes. I make mistakes all the time; I just rebrand them as learning opportunities and build from them. As a Power Brander, you also know that when it comes to the results, if they aren't what you expected or what you wanted, you do take accountability for that as well.

So here is the secret sauce to the Power Brander: You are accountable for the successes and failures; the good comes with the bad. When things don't go as planned, take accountability for taking a look at what happened in order to evaluate how things could've been done differently, as well as accountability for moving yourself, as well as your team, on to the next plateau.

One of the things that is missing, particularly in the business world that we live in, is accountability for things like being truthful, being honest, and living those core values. When you make a mistake—and you often will—as a business professional, or a career professional, as well as an entrepreneur or small business owner, you must own up to those mistakes. Make no excuses, and determine what it is that you need to do to bring your brand—your Power Brand—back in line with you core values as well as your mission.

The bottom line to the power brander is the need to understand the difference between accountability and simple responsibility. If you think about it, what makes that so special for the power brander?

A Power Brander always knows and is keenly aware of the risks and the challenges of the tough assignments that they take on. That separates _you_ from the pack! Your willingness to take on what others are not willing, able, or prepared to tackle—head on—while being accountable for the results.

You're accountable for those activities that your team undertakes as well as—most importantly—you're accountable for the results. This is no zone for someone who wants to point a finger at someone else or believes in excuses. As the saying goes, "When you point a finger at someone else, four of your other fingers point right back at you!"

An added bonus to establishing and living in a zone of accountability is trust. When others see that you hold yourself and your team accountable, the amount of trust in you is built up exponentially. There is no better compliment that can be placed on you than someone or many people saying, "I trust you to say what you do, and do what you say." That is a **Power Brander** in action!

Time to take an honest assessment of where you are on the accountability scale.

- In the last 30 days have you held yourself and your team accountable for the results, good and bad?

- When things did not turn out as planned, did you take accountability for reviewing what caused the missed result?

- Have you clearly explained your and your team's accountability in an empowering and open dialogue?

If the answer to ANY of the questions above was a "No," it's time to step back and determine if you've been living and operating within those core values that you previously defined, or, add accountability to them. Your brand is at stake here, so don't allow that stigma of someone who does the blame game to be connected with you. You have a choice to make: Do you want to have a Power Brand along with the benefits that comes with it or not? Time to take action!

If the answer to ALL of the questions above was a resounding "Yes!" then congratulation, you've conquered one of the most challenging and rewarding power principles of Power Branders!

CHAPTER EIGHT

Relevance

POWER PRINCIPLE: Relevance

The next power principle is called relevance. So what is relevance?

It's defined as "the quality or state of being closely connected or aligned at a given time." So let's break that down.

- The quality or state of being *closely connected*, which means you have to have your ear to the ground (as my grandad used to say) and understand the pulse of what is changing around you in business.

- You have to be able to expand your mind to understand and to seek out what the current state of business within your area or field is.

- The other key concept is at a given time. The speed of change in our society and the world around us, as well as the ever-evolving business environment, is oftentimes mind boggling. This speed of change will make it difficult for you if you do not embrace the concept of relevance to maintain and sustain your Power Brand.

My dad was a decorated war veteran who first introduced me to this concept of relevance back when he was transitioning from his military service into a civil service position.

I remember one day he came home, and he told me and my mom, "I am going to computer school, because that's the way to qualify for the best in high paying jobs that will allow me to leverage my skills from the military, and to provide a better position with some career advancement."

I remember him coming home on a number of different days with stacks of books about these things called computer languages, which I didn't really understand at the time because I was still relatively young and we had no computers in our home. The books had titles like Cobal, Fortran, and some of the other languages that I really didn't have any clue what they were about. All I knew is that these were really thick books that he would come home with and conscientiously study every night.

Soon, he started talking about things called computer cards and tapes, which again I had no clue what he was referring to.

He eventually completed those computer courses and went on to a very distinguished civil service career with the US Postal Service, where he worked until his retirement. Fast forward a few years. I remember going to college and taking a computer course as one of my initial courses as a freshman. I remembered the experience my dad had gone through, so I knew I was ready to get an easy "A" in the course. I arrived to class on the first day, in a room with hundreds of freshmen like myself. Midway through the session, I boldly asked the instructor, "Hey, where are the cards and tapes we'll use for the class?"

As you can probably guess, I got a hysterical laughter from the class, a confusing look from the instructor, and everyone looking at me like I was from another planet. Obviously, I didn't understand the concept of relevance!

As we say in the Navy…"That ship had sailed and I wasn't on it!" I still laugh about that to this day.

Relevance in today's world loves speed. Speed is also one of the most important tools to a Power Brander.

POWER PRINCIPLE: Power Branders study, learn, apply and refine.

Your ability to be relevant depends on:

1. Your desire to be a constant learner

2. Your intent to quickly apply what you learn

3. Your willingness to understand the business environment around you and to be as adaptive as you can to that environment

There really is no excuse why you can't stay ahead of where your particular business or personal development trends are heading strategically. Because we live in an information age, access to knowledge is unlimited. Here are just a few sources to stay current:

- Trade Journals like the Harvard Business Review
- Related Conferences
- Online learning
- Internal / external public courses
- Internet research and interest groups
- Formal learning at Colleges and Universities
- Local business Meetup groups focused on your area of expertise

Caution: Here are some of the pitfalls to staying current.

Number one: being stuck in yesterday's success. At a time when things in our environment are changing so quickly, it is very easy to find something that you're really good at, stay consistent with your approach over the long term of a career, or as your business starts to engage with more and more customers and clients and find yourself and / or your business in a comfort zone. Remember, the environment around you is constantly changing; you have no control over that. The speed of change around you can actually be one of the pitfalls that can damage your brand as well as the brand of your business.

The other pitfall is not predicting when the environment shifts (ex. timing).

Business used to revolve around the ability to be steady, consistent, and predictable. However, with the rate of change and disruption, particularly in technology, in order to be successful you have to embrace those things that are more *lean and agile*. So what do we mean? Lean being the ability to execute very, very quickly, to look at mid-course corrections that are required, and to execute while reducing the amount of waste in your operations. Agility being the ability to rapidly shift and change based on the needs of your business, customers, and external environment.

So here's the exercise. I'd like you to write down three things that show your relevance to what is important in your business or your career. You will have to look outside of the things that you're currently doing today, and do some research to determine what those things are. The main question that you would ask yourself is: What are the three things that I need to understand to ensure that those activities that I do and the way that I execute those activities are relevant in the environment that I currently find myself in and in the future?

In order to enhance your Power Brand, you must commit to remaining current and adapt a lean, agile learning and execution mindset in order to stay relevant!

CHAPTER NINE

Power Networks and Relationships

> **POWER PRINCIPLE: Establish powerful networks and relationships**

Power Branders know that it's very important to establish powerful networks and relationships. So, what does that look like for you as a business professional, entrepreneur, or small business owner?

Let's start with networks. It's often said that your "net worth" is determined by your network, and in many cases that's very true, particularly if you are a business professional, entrepreneur or small business owner, because those networks allow you to expand your reach. Besides the obvious business benefits, they can also provide timely mentorship, candid feedback, and a very important concept—leverage.

One of the easiest ways to begin networking is by attending local or national networking events, Chamber of Commerce meetings, and local Meetups or conferences. The Power Brander does not look at it as just a social gathering, but views it as a way to actively listen and connect with other business professionals that can be sources for expanding both parties' networks, as well as direct partnerships.

How do you effectively network?

A few key steps in networking are:

1. Preparation
2. Attitude / Spirit of giving
3. Authenticity
4. Relationship building

Preparation. Most business professionals I meet at networking events lack the obvious preparation to be effective. In many ways, it's just another one-on-one meeting for coffee, lunch or dinner out. Power Branders (that's you ☺) go beyond the normal routine by:

- Taking the time to know a little bit more about the person or group that they're meeting. PBs realize that a little extra time understanding the other person's needs and wants goes a long way in establishing trust and credibility.

- Being laser focused on what it is that they would also like to get out of the discussion or meeting. You may be thinking, "that's selfish!" at this point, but nothing could be further from the truth. Both parties need to leave feeling it was a win-win interaction.

- Understanding their own brand and how they want it to come out in the meeting or one-on-one conversation.

Attitude / Spirit of Giving. Power Branders view all networking events as an opportunity to share the KSA (Knowledge, Skills, and Abilities) they possess without a lot of hype or under-handed motives. The ratio of giving to receiving is usually tilted toward giving for Power Branders, because they live in a world of abundance. Now, I'm not a psychologist or personal development guru, nor do I pretend to portray one in this book, on the internet, or in social media, but what I've found through experience is that people are attracted to people that they Like, Know, and Trust.

How do you build L-K-T? By authentically giving more than you receive, it's that simple.

Authenticity and relationship building: We discussed this in the chapter on being authentic. For developing powerful networks and relationships, it is just as important, because networking and building relationships is primarily about people. Being authentic gives a signal to the other person that you are a very genuine and approachable person. This approach by Power

Branders leads most people to want to work with you because they know that you can be trusted in situations that are very difficult, or they know that you network well enough that if you don't have the answer, you have a substantial network built on strong relationships that you can reach out to. That is key to being very, very successful in business. It's not only knowing what you know, and being very real about it, and not bragging about things that you don't know, but also being connected with people who you know are one call or email away.

Another key to networking and relationship building is being able to clearly define your own brand and the value it brings. The inevitable question that is always asked:

"Hey, what do you (your business or team) do?", or "Hey, what does your company do?"

That's where we always talk about the 30-second elevator pitch. While it's so important to be able to do that, it's equally as important to frame it so that the receiver(s) can identify their WIIFM—What's in it for me?

Here's a framework that I'm going to give you if someone asks you about what it is that your (feel free to substitute team, company, or business) do?

"Hi, my name is (fill in the blanks)…

I / we (my team, company, business) assists (fill in the blank with target market, internal department, customer, ideal client— ex. entrepreneurs, small business owners, operations department..) with (fill in the blanks—big promise, business results...ex. reducing cost, remaining compliant, increasing sales, reducing software defects, etc..)

by (fill in the blanks –high level "how"—ex. utilizing existing resources, leveraging the internet and social media, outsourcing administrative tasks, creating your personal Power Brand)."

A quick note for career professionals working in established corporations: We've already established the power of building relationships; you have to understand that in our talented business world, it's also very important that you establish both vertical and horizontal relationships. Vertical meaning within your team or larger department / division; horizontal is across different, partner units / teams, particularly if you're working in a company that has teamwork and relationship building as one of the core values.

POWER PRINCIPLE: Power Branders in company settings devote dedicated time to reach up, down, and across the company to foster critical relationships.

So what should you do next?

The first thing to do is to make sure that you make building impactful networks and relationships a priority. Second, ensure you are acting authentic, with genuine intent. No one wants to feel as though they are being taken advantage of or that you're utilizing and leveraging a relationship to take advantage of the situation. The relationship building has to be sincere. It has to be reciprocal, which means if you're going into a business relationship, just as you would with any other type of relationship, it has to be a win-win situation for both parties. Too often what I see from business professionals is trying to get, get, get, and never to give. And so, one of the things that Power Branders do especially well is know how to give first, so that they can receive and reciprocate in time. That's what separates a Power Brander; they are someone who is dynamic and is both confident and competent in the things that they know, so that they can reach out and provide their expertise based on people's trust. And it's simply just about the law of attraction.

Bottom line: when you're establishing these networks, it needs to be both broad and deep. Broad meaning the network covers a number of different areas. Deep meaning you have a number of similar skill sets, department team members, mentors you can tap into when necessary.

Perhaps your network is in operations, marketing, sales, social media, online systems, compliance, regulatory, human resources or accounting. The broader your network is the more you have the ability to be a connector, and that enhances your brand 10X!

Power branders are often great connectors.

We have 30 days, let's get out and make those connections!

CHAPTER TEN

Action

POWER PRINCIPLE: Take Action Now!

Power Branders:

- ✓ Take decisive action in many cases when others don't!

- ✓ Drive for results. I remember what my first manager told me many years ago in a manufacturing company that I was hired into to supervise a production shift (8 hours).

In a really gruff voice, he said, "Walt, let me tell ya...as a supervisor, you get paid for results, not activity." I have to admit, I've used that line everywhere I've worked and in my business to this day.

- ✓ Use speed as a competitive advantage over their competition. Earlier in the book, we talked about lean, agile execution. Power Branders use this to work and execute efficiently.

- ✓ Think strategically. They're Big Picture thinkers and still able to translate that to flawless tactical execution.

- ✓ Always devise a way to GSD (get "shit" done!). They routinely overcome obstacles by seeing them as opportunities without getting into the whine and complain category. They execute with a sense of urgency not panic, which means establishing realistic plans and deadlines that are in line with the goals.

- ✓ Reject the status quo and what others have been doing over and over again. Like a mentor of mine defined insanity, "It's like drinking a bottle of poison and expecting someone else to die."

Caution: Here are some words of caution as you execute on your 30-day plan to build your Power Brand: **Beware of the self-limiting, self-talk that may be going through your mind.**

"I can't build a power brand." One of the reasons a number of people say that is because they believe that it's too hard, takes too long, or there's other self-limiting doubt.

"I'm too young, old, inexperienced."

Breakout Brand:
30 days to your Personal and Business Power Brand

"I'm too settled. I'm too….." You name it.

"I don't have enough time, money, education."

"I don't know enough about …." (Fill in the blanks.)

There will always be things that will stand in your way and try to make you think that you can't do it, but you have everything that you need.

Put the principles in this book to work for you, starting with establishing a firm foundation:

- Unique core values
- A mission larger than you
- Dress for results

Once that foundation is quickly and firmly established, move to the power principles:

- Authenticity
- Accountability
- Relevance
- Power networks and relationships
- Confidence versus competence
- Action—the most important principle!

A key step is making sure that you're operating in an area of intent. You have to declare, "I am committed to developing and growing my Power Brand NOW!"

Knowing with that commitment comes the benefits of freedom, control over your destiny, and the ability to take your business career or your business to new levels of personal and financial success, the next thing is you have to take action—<u>deliberate action.</u>

Carve out time every day for the next 30 days to work on, tweak, improve, and commit to those Power Principles

Remember you have 30 days…so let's get movin'!

CHAPTER ELEVEN

Repairing Brand Damage

At this point I think we need to take a quick step back, and discuss two very serious questions:

- How do I know if my brand is damaged?
- How do I repair my brand if it becomes damaged?

Here are the top four ways that you'll know if your brand or your personal or business brand is in trouble:

1. Number One. If you're a career professional, if you've suddenly stopped being invited to key meetings. Particularly, those meetings that you or your team have been previously been invited to and are active participants. So you stop being invited.

2. Number Two. If you're a career professional and your opinion or your expertise is no longer being sought. **Serious RED flag!** Nobody's coming to you for feedback nor advice in areas you and your colleagues previously considered your area of expertise. Nobody's asking you for your opinion. And certainly once you give it, it's being dismissed.

3. Number Three. Not being included in the strategy planning process. Power branders are always included on strategic meetings or discussions where strategy and focus over a longer term is being discussed. Not necessarily tactical solutions to everyday problems.

4. Number Four. If you're an entrepreneur or a small business owner, let's face it, customers vote with their feet, attention (online), and especially their money. When you start seeing your sales fall off, when you start seeing customer engagement fall off or seeing negative comments on online review sites—**Caution.** When you start seeing customers or clients taking the time and effort to post negative things to social media, your brand is absolutely in trouble!

So why do I mention this? The reason is, if any of these kinds of things are happening to you, or if you get feedback that they're

Breakout Brand:
30 days to your Personal and Business Power Brand

happening to you, then you absolutely have to read and re-read this book. Your 30-day countdown begins today!

This book is written to be easily consumable, but you have to take action because your brand, reputation, career mobility, or business profitability may be at stake already!

What if you find yourself in any of the situations listed above?

Here are the steps to take immediately!

1. Face it head on and determine if you can recover—if things have gotten this far someone has lost faith in your competence or is not confident that you can deliver results. It may be a supervisor or co-worker, perhaps your clients if you are an entrepreneur or business owner and you see dramatic drops in your sales and profits.

2. Prepare yourself for direct feedback.

3. Find your trusted advisor within your network.

4. Read each chapter of this book carefully and honestly commit to the action plans.

5. Make an accelerated plan (to gain back trust and confidence or position yourself to move to another opportunity).

6. Take Action Now!

First, you have to be self-aware enough to know when this is going on, or you need to be connected to someone, perhaps a peer or mentor, who can give you some honest, uncensored feedback of where you are.

Next, **seek feedback from another Power brander**. These mentors, as you're going to find out, are very self-aware as well as aware of the environment around them, and are very well connected. They'll know if, in fact, there's something wrong with your brand.

If you're an entrepreneur, connect with other entrepreneurs and get feedback from those who can go through your sales funnel, who can give you feedback on how user-friendly your brand is, and where you actually stand versus similar competitors.

Make a list of how you got to where you are. What was the underlying cause to get you here from where you were? Then, at the end of the day, you have a serious decision to make.

You have to be willing to press the reset button, and then ask yourself honestly, is this situation salvageable?

If the answer is yes, please do yourself a HUGE favor....go back to the chapter in this book where we discuss core values, your mission statement and go through the exercise with a **sense of urgency**!

Time is not on your side!

You have got to get your Brand back into a healthy state before it's too late.

If the answer is no, then you're basically saying that the situation is not salvageable. Then, you need to ask yourself some other questions. Do I need a new situation? For example, if you're a career professional, ask yourself, do I need to change to a different unit, to a different division—if, in fact, you want to stay in the same company—or do I actually need to start looking at other companies after I go through my brand makeover?

The bottom line to you is, once you're in a situation like this, it will take an effort from you to get yourself in the right situation. My strong recommendation to you is that you go through the exercises in this book to get yourself into a position that you can regain the power of your brand and the resulting benefits that it gives you!

At this point, it's definitely a **SPRINT** and you have to get moving!

CHAPTER TWELVE

Bonus! How to Turbocharge your Power Brand

There's actually a number of ways that you can turbocharge your power brand and take it to a higher level than you can with the foundational elements found throughout this book. Make no mistake, if you take action and apply the Power Brand principles found within this book, you **will** be more successful. These are items that I've personally tried, tested, and have been successful over time. Which means they'll never go out of style, become ineffective, or be superseded by other business and development "stuff."

There's actually three other ways that I've found that will turbocharge or accelerate your power brand.

1. The first way is to be generous and give back to your community. If you haven't figured it out to this point: **Power Branders are servant leaders** who want to help out, particularly in their community, by feeding the hungry, volunteering at the local food bank, religious, civic organization, or shelter that supports feeding those who are less fortunate. I'm particularly passionate about caring for homeless veterans.

   Perhaps it's donating time; donate clothing or money to a local or national cause. That also helps people that are in need. Or you can do things like volunteer to be a reader to younger children at their schools. Power Branders turbocharge their brand by being out in the community and being visible. I'm not talking about going out and giving speeches, but about being out there so that people know that you care about your community.

2. Start your own nonprofit company or make a decision to devote a certain percentage or certain dollar amount of sales to a cause that you support.

   What it shows is that that you're expanding upon your core values and you're actually getting to live out your mission which many other people would love to do if they were in your situation. Power Branders who are business owners are well aware of what impact they can have on their community and beyond.

3. **Write your own best-selling book!** There is no more powerful way of turbocharging your Power Brand than to

write and publish (notice I said write AND publish!) your own **best-selling book**.

Why?

- You are automatically seen as the expert and authority in your field.

- It is a great leverage point for your career and your business.

- It opens up doors and greater career options---remember one of the key benefits for establishing a Power Brand---Options!

- You can build a marketing platform for your business.

- It's part of your Power Brand legacy.

According to estimates, over 80% of people want to write a book but only 1% of people actually write and publish books. Go ahead and ask your friends, associates, and other people you know if they would love to write and publish a book.

So obviously there's a gap between wanting to write a book and the ability to write a book and then for that book to be a best seller. Let me give you some of the steps that it takes to take a book to number one bestseller.

You need to:

- Have an idea for a book. My suggestion is a non-fiction book about business, relationships, personal or leadership development, software development, or whatever your area of expertise happens to be in.

Newsflash: 80% plus of people have some idea what they would write about but only 1% does anything about it!

- Create a compelling cover and title—first impressions matter.

- Commit to writing and publishing it in less than 60 days! If you don't, your desire to do so will eventually fade.

- Find a good editor and proofreader, particularly if you're like me and not the most scholarly author. Someone who can refine the worst that you actually put on the page and do the layout so it's easy to read.

- Determine which platform you want to publish the book on—I strongly recommend Amazon Kindle FIRST!
    - Then publish as a physical book
    - Eventually publish as an audio book

- Build some momentum for the book sales---the "secret sauce."

- Establish a marketing platform to leverage the book's popularity for you and your business.

For most it seems a bit daunting, but not YOU—you are a Power Brander!

*If you need help with writing and publishing your number one best seller, check out the resources on our author page or email me directly: Coaching@WaltLaurel.com

Time to get it in motion and turbo-charge your Power Brand!

COACHING AND CONSULTING

A Note from the Author

One of the fastest ways to explode your business and accelerate your career is getting advice from someone who's been there, done that, and has already gone down the road you would like to travel. In our dynamic business world, results have to be obtained <u>quickly</u> and they have to be <u>sustained</u>. We can assist in those key areas.

Caution: I am very selective with whom we choose to work with and only offer premium services which may be considered very expensive for some potential clients. However, if you are the right fit, I will leverage my and my team's experience to get you (career professionals) and business owners "no fluff," bottom line results!

Here are some of the areas we can work together on:

- Lead generation and viral marketing
- Content creation
- Leveraging speaking engagements for greater profitability
- How to do your own live or virtual events
- Interviewing strategies for career professionals
- Personal and small business branding strategies
- Creating processes and systems in your business to drive efficient and effective bottom-line results
- Podcasting and radio show hosting
- Publicity and media attention
- Becoming a number one best-selling author *(hint, you're reading one right now!)*
- Marketing automation
- Outsourcing

This list is not exhaustive, so you might want to reach out to my team to come up with a strategic plan to help you boost your career or for you business owners and entrepreneurs, to double your revenue.

If you're interested in consulting with me please shoot me an email: **coaching@WaltLaurel.com**.

ABOUT THE AUTHOR

Walt Laurel is a leadership and performance consultant, business coach, keynote speaker and best-selling author. After graduating with a Bachelor's degree in Engineering, he served 10 years of distinguished servant leadership as a US Naval Officer, attaining the designations of Surface Warfare Officer (SWO) and Engineering Officer.

After leaving the Navy, he has 20+ years of leadership experience with a number of Fortune 500 internationally known brands, including Johnson & Johnson, Gillette, and Avery Dennison. Always the serial entrepreneur and leadership coach, he is the owner of Laurel Consulting Group and Passion Driven Marketing, whose mission is to empower business leaders and entrepreneurs with the ability to build their personal brand, leadership acumen, and increase business profitability.

Email: Support@PassionDrivenMarketing.com

www.ingramcontent.com/pod-product-compliance
Lightning Source LLC
Chambersburg PA
CBHW071412220526
45469CB00004B/1263